News Crew

Level 6 – Orange

Helpful Hints for Reading at Home

The graphemes (written letters) and phonemes (units of sound) used throughout this series are aligned with Letters and Sounds. This offers a consistent approach to learning, whether reading at home or in the classroom.

HERE IS A LIST OF PHONEMES FOR THIS PHASE OF LEARNING. AN EXAMPLE OF THE PRONUNCIATION CAN BE FOUND IN BRACKETS.

Phase 5			
ay (day)	ou (out)	ie (tie)	ea (eat)
oy (boy)	ir (girl)	ue (blue)	aw (saw)
wh (when)	ph (photo)	ew (new)	oe (toe)
au (Paul)	a_e (make)	e_e (these)	i_e (like)
o_e (home)	u_e (rule, cube)		

Phase 5 Alternative Pronunciations of Graphemes			
a (hat, what)	e (bed, she)	i (fin, find)	o (hot, so, other)
u (but, unit)	c (cat, cent)	g (got, giant)	ow (cow, blow)
ie (tied, field)	ea (eat, bread)	er (farmer, herb)	ch (chin, school, chef)
y (yes, by, very)	ou (out, shoulder, could, you)		

HERE ARE SOME WORDS WHICH YOUR CHILD MAY FIND TRICKY.

Phase 5 Tricky Words			
oh	their	people	Mr
Mrs	looked	called	asked
could			

TOP TIPS FOR HELPING YOUR CHILD TO READ:

• Allow children time to break down unfamiliar words into units of sound and then encourage children to string these sounds together to create the word.

• Encourage your child to point out any focus phonics when they are used.

• Read through the book more than once to grow confidence.

• Ask simple questions about the text to assess understanding.

• Encourage children to use illustrations as prompts.

This book focuses on /u_e, /ue/ and /ew/ and is an Orange level 6 book band.

Can you sort all the words on this page into two groups?

Brew

Tune

Words with u_e

Mule

New

Cure

Words with ew

Dew

Cube

Do you ever think about the people who tell us the news? They have an important job. They help us understand what is happening around us.

There are a few different jobs in a news crew. There are lots of people that we do not see on the TV screen.

Some people tell the news. They explain true things that have happened to us. When they are on air, they must not panic.

They might read a screen with cues on it so they do not forget what to say. They must speak in a clear way.

Cue screen

Some people tell us when it is going to rain or be hot. They can tell us if a storm is near.

On the TV, we see them pointing at a map. However, they have to point at a green screen without looking.

Some people have the job of getting it all on film. They use a lens to film the people we see on TV.

They might film in the news room. They might go out to film an event at a new spot each day.

There are people in the news crew who help come up with what to say on air. They make sure that the crew just tells us things that are true.

Some people tell the crew what to do. They choose which parts of the film to use and which parts to exclude.

Exclude means to take out.

Staying on top of the most current news can be a big job. To do it well, the crew has to act as a team.

All the people in a news crew have value. Without them, we might never hear what is happening around the planet. Thank you, news crew!

©2023 **BookLife Publishing Ltd.**
King's Lynn, Norfolk, PE30 4LS, UK.

ISBN 978-1-80505-083-4

All rights reserved. Printed in China.
A catalogue record for this book is
available from the British Library.

News Crew
Written by Charis Mather
Designed by Isabella Croker

An Introduction to BookLife Readers…

Our Readers have been specifically created in line with the London Institute of Education's approach to book banding and are phonetically decodable and ordered to support each phase of the Letters and Sounds document.

Each book has been created to provide the best possible reading and learning experience. Our aim is to share our love of books with children, providing both emerging readers and prolific page-turners with beautiful books that are guaranteed to provoke interest and learning, regardless of ability.

BOOK BAND GRADED using the Institute of Education's approach to levelling.

PHONETICALLY DECODABLE supporting each phase of Letters and Sounds.

EXERCISES AND QUESTIONS to offer reinforcement and to ascertain comprehension.

CLEAR DESIGN to inspire and provoke engagement, providing the reader with clear visual representations of each non-fiction topic.

AUTHOR INSIGHT:
CHARIS MATHER

Charis Mather is a children's author at BookLife Publishing who has a love for reading and writing. Her studies in linguistics and experiences working with young readers have given her a knack for writing material that suits a range of ages and skill levels. Charis is passionate about producing books that emphasise the fun in reading and is convinced that no matter how much you already know, there is always something new to learn.

This book focuses on /u_e/, /ue/ and /ew/ and is an Orange level 6 book band.

Image Credits Images are courtesy of Shutterstock.com. With thanks to Getty Images, Thinkstock Photo and iStockphoto. Cover – michaeljung, Funtap, Aggapom Poomitud, indigo_design. p4-5 – Grusho Anna, Gorodenkoff. p6-7 – withGod, Krakenimages.com. p8-9 – Thomas Andreas, Gorodenkoff. p10-11 – jan kranendonk, Billion Photos. p12-13 – SpeedKingz, REALDEE. p14-15 – Omeer, GaudiLab.